Winter

by Gail Saunders-Smith

Content Consultant:
Lisa M. Nyberg, Ph.D.
Educator, Springfield (Oregon) Public Schools

an imprint of Capstone Press

1

Pebble Books

Pebble Books are published by Capstone Press
818 North Willow Street, Mankato, Minnesota 56001
http://www.capstone-press.com

Library of Congress Cataloging-in-Publication Data
Saunders-Smith, Gail.
    Winter/by Gail Saunders-Smith.
    p. cm.
    Includes bibliographical references and index.
    Summary: Simple text and photographs depict the weather, plants, animals, and activities of winter.
    ISBN 1-56065-784-7
    1. Winter—Juvenile literature. [1. Winter.] I. Title.
    QB637.8.S28 1998
    508.2—dc21   98-5043
                                                                          CIP
                                                                          AC

Note to Parents and Teachers

This book describes and illustrates the changes in weather, people, plants, and animals in winter. The close picture-text matches support early readers in understanding the text. The text offers subtle challenges with compound and complex sentence structures. This book also introduces early readers to expository and content-specific vocabulary. The expository vocabulary is defined in the Words to Know section. Early readers may need assistance in reading some of these words. Readers also may need assistance in using the Table of Contents, Words to Know, Read More, Internet Sites, and Index/Word List sections of the book.

2

Table of Contents

Winter is a season for resting. Winter comes after autumn and before spring.

The northern and central parts of North America have cold weather. Some places may have blizzards. Blizzards are storms with strong winds and a lot of snow. People must wear heavy coats and hats to stay warm.

The southern part of North America usually does not have snow during winter. Temperatures there may be cooler in winter than in summer. But the weather usually is still warm. People do not need to wear heavy clothing.

Snow and cold weather bring different things to do. People need to shovel snow off sidewalks and streets. People also play in the snow. They go ice skating and sledding.

Some people take vacations. People who live in colder places may visit warmer places. Other people may go to the mountains to ski and snowboard.

Many trees lose their
leaves before winter.
They stop making food.
They stop growing. They
rest and wait for spring
to come.

Most plants rest too. Their roots and seeds are under the soil. They wait for warm weather to start growing.

18

Animals work harder to find food during winter. Deer push away snow to find grass and twigs. Squirrels dig up nuts and seeds. They hid this food during autumn.

Some animals hibernate during winter. Bears sleep in dens. Bats sleep in caves. They do not eat much during winter. Winter is a season for resting.

Words to Know

blizzard—a winter storm with strong winds and a lot of snow

hibernate—to sleep through winter

mountain—a high, rocky piece of land; some mountains have snow on their tops all year long.

season—one of the four parts of a year; spring, summer, autumn, and winter

ski—to slide over snow while wearing a long piece of wood, metal, or plastic on each foot

sledding—to ride on a wood or plastic vehicle and slide down a snowy hill

snowboard—to slide down a snowy hill while standing on a board

temperature—how hot or cold something is

vacation—a trip away from home

Read More

Anholt, Catherine and Laurence. *Sun, Snow, Stars, Sky.* New York: Viking, 1995.

Gibbons, Gail. *The Reasons for Seasons.* New York: Holiday House, 1995.

Schweninger, Ann. *Wintertime.* Let's Look at the Seasons. New York: Puffin Books, 1993.

 # Internet Sites

Signs of the Seasons
http://www.4seasons.org.uk/projects/seasons/index.html

Snow
http://web.syr.edu/~wrt405/normal/snow.html

❄️ Index/Word List

Word Count: 240
Early-Intervention Level: 12

Editorial Credits

Lois Wallentine, editor; Timothy Halldin, designer; Michelle L. Norstad, photo researcher

Photo Credits

Cheryl R. Richter, 12
Chuck Place, 14
Dembinsky Photo Associates/Mark E. Gibson, cover
James P. Rowan, 4, 20
Richard Hamilton Smith, 1, 6, 16
Root Resources/Stan Osolinski, 18
Unicorn Stock Photos/Jeff Greenberg, 8; Jim Shippee, 10